A. _____ ayer

by
Mary Charles-Murray S.N.D.

*All booklets are published thanks to the
generous support of the members of the
Catholic Truth Society*

CATHOLIC TRUTH SOCIETY
PUBLISHERS TO THE HOLY SEE

Contents

1. Introduction 3

II. Accessibility to the Spirit 10

III. Looking at the Author of the Faith 32

IV. Conclusion 53

1. Introduction

True Christianity

In 1603 in Amsterdam the Catholic artist, THEODORE GALLE produced an engraving illustrating how to be a true Christian. Since being a true Christian means to imitate Christ, he thought the best way to sum this up was to depict Christ carrying his cross as a model for artists. He added at the top of his picture an apt quotation from the Epistle to the Hebrews (*Heb* 12:2) which translates as – "looking at the Author of the Faith".

At the bottom of his picture he inscribes another quotation, which he attributes to St Augustine, that a person bears the name of Christian in vain if he or she only imitates Christ in a very minimal way. So how we see Christ will actually be how we engage with him, and this will be an individual and personal experience.

To imitate Christ then first of all we have to look at him closely. So Galle continues his idea by showing that only one artist, the one immediately opposite Christ, is copying the model realistically. The other artists have different visions of what they see, and are painting various scenes from his life, in some cases recognisably based on the New Testament. In other words they are interpreting the model. We have here then two kinds of imitation, artistic imitation and personal imitation, intimately linked together, and the engraving encapsulates wonderfully the theme of this booklet: the relationship of art and prayer; or, to put it another way, art and personal spirituality. Union with Christ in prayer comes from close, personal observation of him.

Art and Catholic identity

To place art in relation to prayer and spirituality in this manner is a distinctly Catholic way of understanding Christian wisdom, and of understanding the true Wisdom who is the Author of the faith. Being a Catholic means to have certain ways of talking and thinking about Christianity which are characteristic, and one of these ways is talking and thinking through images.

Art for Catholics is a deeply religious matter because religion permeates the whole of life; and it is by means primarily of art that we, as human beings, try to see things as they really are. While science seeks to understand the world in terms of investigating empirical evidence and solving practical problems, art seeks to move to something beyond knowledge and demonstration to try and reach meaning and

Christ carrying the cross as a model for painters.
Engraving by Theodore Galle from Johann David's
Veridicus Christianus Amsterdam, 1603. Rijksmuseum,
Amsterdam. Cat.no. 23.

significance. The question of art and its relationship to prayer presents us with a case study in Catholic identity as it relates to the imagination.

It is not surprising then that in an address to artists on May 7th 1964 Pope Paul VI lamented publicly the estrangement of the Church from the artistic world. In the carefully chosen setting of the Sistine Chapel underneath Michelangelo's great frescoes, he blamed to some extent the Church itself for failing to understand the visions of the present. And he appealed for a restoration of friendship, so that the Church could once again take advantage of the language that art offers for understanding ourselves and our experience. Above all he wanted art to make accessible once again the world of the spirit, which is the world of prayer. As he put it, echoing the words of Pope Gregory the Great, "...in this operation of expressing the invisible world of the spirit in accessible, intelligible terms, you (artists) are the masters."

The Pope's views were formalized at the Second Vatican Council in the document on the liturgy, *Sacrosanctum Concilium* (nn.122-130). As far as the Church is concerned therefore the central place of art in the living of the Christian life has been unequivocally reaffirmed. According to papal and conciliar teaching, art by its nature gives access to the life of prayer.

Art and artistic identity

From the artistic side a reply in the form of an appreciation of the Pope's initiative was written by the distinguished art critic, Sir John Rothenstein, who pointed out that the collapse of the friendship between art and religion was not wholly the Church's fault, since for the last century and a half an assumption had grown up that art was an entirely autonomous activity which referred to nothing outside itself. And he further pointed out that the alienation of the artist from the Church was only part of a wider alienation of the artist from society as a whole. Since in his view the functions once exercised by artists had been taken over by photographers and journalists, artists had retreated into art simply considered as art. And this, he thought, accounted for the almost dominant preoccupation with abstraction as the leading form of art for most of the 20th century.

While Rothenstein's analysis of serious art today - as having in general a conspicuously private, rather than a public character - might make difficulties for the public art of the Church, paradoxically it may well make it an aid rather than a hindrance to the private prayer with which we are concerned. And in bringing art to our prayer we are not only looking at Christ and repairing the friendship between art and the Church, but also helping to re-establish the relationship between art and society.

Art and theological identity

Historically, it was the early Church that set up a Christian artistic sensibility, based on the Bible, by promulgating the idea that there is a continuity of physical and spiritual things, and it is the image which forms the bridge between them. But, although both the Eastern and the Western Church agree in finding in the image the natural bridge to prayer, they differ with regard to its nature. Unlike the Eastern Church, with its liturgical and spiritualized conception of the icon, the controlling influence on the understanding of art and prayer for the West was not the liturgy but the Bible. The western tradition of art is essentially Gospel orientated in its thinking and in subject matter.

Stylistically Christian art began with the advantage of a mature artistic tradition, that of the ancient world, which it then recast in accordance with the Gospel, while still retaining the contemporary cultural forms. This initial transformation of inherited forms has resulted throughout its history in a constant understanding by the Western Church, in contradiction to the theology of the icon, that cultural and artistic styles may and must change in order to clarify current thinking concerning Christ and his people.

Theologically art was established on the concept of the doctrine of Genesis and that of the book of

Wisdom, that the human person is made in the image of God. This concern for the biblical teaching on the image introduced into early Christian thinking a preoccupation with the body; and an interest in its structures, senses and functions and its relationship to its natural environment, which has constantly informed the western tradition ever since. One of the great themes of western art has always been the human body, and it owes this interest originally to early Christian adoptions of, and modifications on the classical artistic tradition in the interest of the biblical text.

Accordingly in respect of prayer, accessibility to the spirit begins from below, from our embodied lives, and thence moves upwards to God. The physical and the metaphysical are joined through the images of art, which provide us theologically, psychologically and graphically with a means to express this accessibility in an ever changing and unusual language. Physicality, image and spirit are thus intertwined.

II. Accessibility to the Spirit

Art and human reality

St Julie Billiart once described prayer as "one only soul to one only God". And St Augustine in his *Soliloquies* (Sol.I.1) put it another way, when he said that there are only two subjects worthwhile for human consideration, God and the human being. If we look at the history of art we find that these are the subjects which have pre-eminently occupied artists. This is one of the reasons therefore why art, as well as being intimately connected with prayer, also provides subjects for it. Many saints, such as St John Chrysostom and St Ignatius Loyola are recorded as beginning their prayer with the contemplation of an artistic image, since both forms of expression are dealing with the same fundamentals; and what these fundamentals are is displayed in the earliest Christian image we possess.

The Orans figure

The continuity of the physical and spiritual is exemplified in the much debated *Orans* (praying)

Donna Velata. Cubiculum of the Velatio, Catacomb of Priscilla. Rome, 4th Century.

figures of the catacomb and early sarcophagal art. They depict the real meaning and significance of the human being. The orans figure is a human person, male or female, shown fully frontal, often with the eyes, which are huge, upraised to heaven, and with the arms outstretched in the ancient attitude of prayer. This idea of frontality and the stress on the largeness of the eyes is deliberate, and it is an extreme development by Christian art of elements found to a lesser degree in Greco-Roman art, such as the portraits from the Faiyum in Egypt. By the fourth-century, as the picture of the so-called *Donna Velata* shows, the impact of the figures comes almost entirely from the eyes, which were held to be the vehicle of the soul.

This representation tells us what the life of the spirit is in general terms: it is a life of total simplicity, because the life of prayer and the true human life are identical. The point of the images is to emphasize for us the nature and importance of prayer. For the early Church what defines us as human beings and Christians, no matter who we are, is our relationship to God. And we are most fully ourselves when we are praying.

These images were created in the third-century A.D. when Christian art appears for the first time in its own right, and they are ubiquitous. They are found in paintings and in sculpture on the related sarcophagi, on gold-glass, in manuscript illustration, on jewellery and on plaques executed in ivory; and they continue on into the 5th century. All human beings are shown in the same typical posture. They are ordinary people whose names are inscribed beside them, such as five year old Felix, or teenage Bessula. But so important are these figures, which describe human nature in its relationship with God, that biblical personages also, such as Daniel, Noah, Susanna and the three Hebrews in the fiery furnace, martyrs like Agnes, and even Christ himself are depicted in the same way. The importance of these images for any consideration of the relationship of art and prayer cannot be overemphasized by reason of their antiquity, style and theological message.

Theological anthropology

Because of their artistic form the ancient images are, as we can see, to some extent generic representations rather than individual portraits. They are concerned to emphasize the general as well as individual: to show us that our relationship to God and prayer comes through our common possession of a common human nature. In this way they provide in a unique, visual manner a theological and objective justification for prayer since they express what is technically called theological anthropology. Our very nature demands prayer. This imaginative leap, made by the earliest Christian artists centuries ago, proved to be a fruitful intellectual matrix for the further evolution of artistic forms, which have been elaborated continuously ever since, and which have deepened further our understanding of life with God.

In the fifteenth-century for example **ALBRECHT DURER** offered his own reflections on prayer and the human person, not by portraying the full human being, but simply by focusing on a part of the body – the hands. Executed by an artist of immense innovation and technical skill, the so-called *Praying Hands*, a brush drawing on blue paper, is one of the most famous of Durer's works. Though it has actually become detached from its original context (as one of the preliminary studies for the Heller altarpiece) it stands now as an autonomous image in its own right, and as an artwork of iconic status. It has come to be regarded especially since the twentieth-century as the symbol and indeed the embodiment of prayer.

Durer was a man of deep religious perceptions much affected by the conflicts of the Reformation, and his works reflect a strong and very personal adherence to Christ. They seek to depict a faith which does not give way in the face of suffering: indeed his last self-portrait, *Self-Portrait in a Fur-Collared Robe*, shows himself as

Albrecht Dürer, Study of an Apostle's Hands (Praying Hands).
Graphische Sammlung, Albertina, Vienna.

Christ the man of sorrows. Like Galle's woodcut, this too speaks of the imitation of Christ, but here to the point of self-identification. It is this which is indicated in a different way in the more generalised picture of the *Hands*.

These hands represent human lives with all their hardships, which are brought to God in prayer. Nevertheless the essence of the image is one of composure. Though hands are made for activity, and these belong to an older man who has known hard work, as the raised veins and sinews show, and who, as indicated by the bent right little finger, possibly suffers arthritis, when they close in prayer they come to rest. Starting with a simple black line, and from the single position of a single object, Dürer produces a deceptively simple image, but one which offers his observer far more than the drawing of a part of the human body. The blue colour of the background reinforces the sense of mental and physical resolution: a hard life, remade in Christ through prayer, is brought to peace in God. The narrative power conveyed through this single, specific image is hard to exaggerate. A life laden with action is transformed in the withdrawal of prayer. The image is not merely an aid to prayer but is a very powerful commentary on its nature.

Vincent Van Gogh, Shoes, 1886. Van Gogh Museum, Amsterdam.

Prayer and the ordinary

Later still in the nineteenth-century, **VINCENT VAN GOGH** extended and modulated the theological idea of human existence by leaving out entirely the human being who owned them, and showing us only his shoes. Unlike the *Orans* representations and Dürer's *Praying Hands*, Van Gogh's image is very highly focused. It inserts into the idea of prayer the importance of the personal daily life of the individual. For Van Gogh what constitutes human identity is not the mere fact of being human, but the daily practices of ordinary life. And since for many people daily life is a struggle, it is the poignancy of the chosen artistic subject, and the artistic form in which it is described, that resonates immensely with us. Prayer relates our ordinary life to God, and God being Truth is therefore found in the truth of our ordinary everyday lives. In the images of both Durer and Van Gogh we are shown a life which has been particularly unexceptional and hard. They illustrate perfectly Kierkegaard's dictum that God never deceives; that is why he is found in the ordinary. Henry Moore, the great British sculptor, also once asked how do you tell a Madonna and Child from a mother and a baby, and the answer is that to some extent you cannot. We learn here that prayer and the ordinary are the same thing.

Art and the nature of prayer

The Church's view that art by its nature gives access to the life of prayer, and the images which we have considered so far, provide us with a perspective for consideration which may act as a corrective of a current and very common mistake, which many commentators have observed, concerning the nature of prayer. Because of the dominant nature of the ascetic tradition, which has been very powerful in matters of spirituality until quite recently, we have inherited an unconscious tendency to identify the life of prayer with a life of good behaviour: one concerned with achieving high ideals. While this is good, and we tend to identify ourselves with our ideals, in reality our lives are more realistically characterised as a struggle between our ideals and our reality. What the images above have shown us is that what we do and should bring to God in prayer is ourselves as we really are, not as we should like to be.

Art therefore can become one of the most powerful forces which can help us to shape our life spiritually. The spirituality that art creates for us is an individual culture of life, a structured shape which can become the most basic feature of our human existence. If with the help of meaningful images we shape our lives and give them the form which is good for us then we experience ourselves not simply as moral persons but as Christians truly alive; possessors of a personal individuality, which appears in a personal self-presentation. Images do this by helping us initially to analyse our thoughts and feelings, and to deal with our own passions and experiences. Art and prayer are thus really both part of the mystical tradition of thinking. Both lead to transcendence, to the mystery of the human being and to the mystery of God, since mysticism, broadly speaking, is a primordial longing to live for God.

The meeting of the divine and the human in Baroque art

Though many artists offer reflections on what they do, and great art has a wide ranging application, it is not in itself theoretical. It is normally related to a given situation, and so the choice of images for personal prayer is usually addressing a concrete case. This is so in the instance of one of the most celebrated artistic commentaries on mysticism as the idea of longing for God, and the mystical nature of prayer as self-transcendence: that great masterpiece of Baroque art, **GIANLORENZO BERNINI'S** sculpture of the ecstasy of St Teresa (1647) in the Cornaro chapel of Santa Maria della Vittoria in Rome.

One dimension of God is of a mystery so awful in its brightness that we imagine him as dwelling far away

Bernini, St Teresa in Ecstasy, Cornaro Chapel, Santa Maria della Vittoria.

and remote from us. And often in this connection we think of the great mystics who have written on prayer as in some way highly privileged having entered this dimension. We find too that so extraordinary are the experiences they sometimes record concerning their prayer that we consider that they are also too remote from our experience to be of real help. But for Bernini, the greatest sculptor of the 17th century and one of the most creative sculptors of all time, Teresa (1515-1582) illustrated prayer in itself and for all. She was not simply the example of an unusual and highly favoured individual. And since he was from 1623 practically in command of the official art policy of the papacy, and his work dominated later European developments, his conception of prayer has to that extent a generalised as well as a particular authority.

In this sculpture, in which he analyses the intellectual and emotional effect of prayer on the person who prays, he summarizes his view of prayer as both immanence and transcendence; albeit that he chooses to represent this in its most extreme form.

The narrative behind the image is that part of St Teresa's autobiography in which she describes her experience of a vision during prayer. Bernini illustrates the moment when Teresa is pierced by God's love, in the guise an angel who plunges a flaming spear into her heart.

On the altar of the chapel a statuary group of white Carrara marble shows the smiling angel and Teresa who is borne prone in ecstasy on a cloud. She is beyond gravity, her eyes are closed and her mouth open. The folds of her robes move with a life, which make visible the impulses of her soul. As in the case of the Orans figures, the human figure is re-appropriated by Bernini to communicate narrative, emotion and meaning. We see and share an episode in the historical life of a particular person, but also in an incident whose meaning is eternal. It is a visual example of what T.S.Eliot described as a moment that "bisects" time. The value of the sculpture for our understanding of prayer lies in this capture of the historical, while at the same time penetrating into its significance. In a highly sensual yet highly intellectual appeal to the viewer, it makes visible the paradox of the immanent and transcendent nature of all prayer.

Art, style and text

The Baroque style, of which this is known as the quintessential image, was powerful and emotional. Derived in part from the theatre, it was intended to produce by means of an extraordinary realism in detail and texture, the most striking dramatic effect possible. And since the general religious purpose of Baroque art was to show the meeting of the divine and the human in the life of all the faithful, so here in the hands of an artist like Bernini, the spectacular realism of the style, with the figures so completely engaged in the events in which they are involved, makes an overwhelming impact on the viewer.

Bernini had well understood that the point of St Teresa's text was more than simply autobiographical. It was intended to teach that the transformation of the soul by love takes place in anyone who lives a steady life of prayer. And that is why the contemporary *Catechism of the Catholic Church* (2709) also quotes St Teresa's definition when dealing with prayer. She writes: "Contemplative prayer in my opinion is nothing else than a close sharing between friends; it means taking time frequently to be alone with him who we know loves us."

While in order to make his impact, Bernini's portrayal may show this idea at its most visceral, and the sculpture may seem to be an almost over-graphic account, nevertheless it represents the transformation which takes place in each of us; and of what happens at every level of prayer. God's action is always the same; He acts on all in prayer in an equally intensified and personal way, but in differing degrees, and in a manner adapted to our own circumstances. The text and the art work match each other. Like St Teresa's own account, the statuary group is basically an analysis of love, applying equally to all who pray.

Art, mysticism and mystery

This idea of access to the spirit by means of the visual expression of the mystical tradition has been recently revisited and re-appropriated in art, often in the form of a commentary on mystery. It has become a rising theme particularly in contemporary art, although different times require different images. The development began in the 20th century with certain painters such as **MARK ROTHKO** and **BARNETT NEWMAN**, and is being continued in the 21st century in the work of skilled practitioners such as **BILL VIOLA**, probably the most celebrated of the current video artists.

Mark Rothko (1903-1970), a Russian-Jewish intellectual and one of the most important painters of the period after World War II, belongs to that generation of American artists who effected a fundamental change in the essence and design of abstract painting. Officially called "color field painting," and often using a dark palette, his pictures are not in any way figurative but are simply formations of pure colour. And since Rothko believed that tragedy and ecstasy were the basic conditions of existence, his intention in creating was to express the dramatic nature of all human life, and for this reason his work is often described as Baroque.

At the heart of his conception is the relationship of the painting to the observer. His aim was that nothing should stand between the painting and the viewer and the exchange that takes place between them. And it is the colour which both provides the emotional force and also the vehicle for the experience. As has been remarked, in these paintings the recipient and the work are merged beyond any verbal comprehension. Their meditative aspect help us to understand that prayer can be simply presence, one only soul to one only God.

Barnett Newman (1905- 1970), like Rothko another of the foremost color field painters, was also a critic and a writer; and, like Rothko was publicly associated with religious themes. He spoke of the seemingly insane drive of man to be painter and poet, and thought that it reflected a desire to return to the Garden of Eden, the scene of the original creation. To create is part of being human, and so art and religion are intimately related.

Video art as sublime experience

Bill Viola (1951-), is one of the leading and most influential artists of the present day, who has achieved international status by establishing video installation as a vital artistic form. In his work technological developments have been put to use to develop the artistic tradition in a unique way, and one which has proved to be immensely popular with the general public. The video technique, once largely the province of the documentary, has become a form which is completely new, in that it emphasises now not so much the record but the purely immediate and existential experience. It is a medium in which the image, instead of being an artistic object, becomes a way of thinking in which it is impossible to tell the real from the illusory. The appeal is simple, common-place, universal and readily understood. It promotes reflection by the direct exercise of the both the logical and the emotional faculties.

Viola's installations have been described as complete surroundings which enwrap the viewer in image, movement and sound, and are distinguished for their directness and ease of understanding. It is because they become engulfed in the totality of the experience offered to its viewers, that his work is frequently referred to as sublime.

Bill Viola's work is also closely connected to the contemporary search for spirituality. And in this way it is concerned to challenge that element, found in much in modern art, which privileges the idea of concept. It has been noted that this is high art for ordinary, contemporary people; and seeing in this way represents a return to an older, narrative rather than a modern, critical viewpoint.

In it he creates a rich video imagery of general appeal in which certain quite core traditional elements, such as water, landscapes animals and human figures, recur; and they are usually displayed very slowly. For this reason, like prayer, they require attentiveness and a certain personal humility in order to enter the experience. And like prayer they can induce a sense of calm in the observer. Characteristic is the installation made in 1996 for Durham Cathedral called *The Messenger*, where motifs of diving and floating recur. A man is shown repeatedly rising from water; he inhales and sinks back in a recurring slow cycle, inevitably inviting associations with Baptism.

The videos are universally agreed to be in some way concerned to make large statements about human life and the human soul, in its relation to nature, death and prayer. And they make use of both the Eastern and Western spiritual traditions, and in particular Christian mysticism. In *Room for St John of the Cross* made in 1983 the mystical tradition is directly referred to and reinterpreted. There is again a return to the idea of immanence and transcendence, but because of the nature of the medium, mystical experience is made real in a way very different way from its treatment in marble by Bernini.

Original drawing of the crucifixion by St John of the Cross. D.R./
Monastery of the Incarnation, Avila.

St John of the Cross as artistic inpiration
for Viola and Dali

St John of the Cross (1542-1591) was a Spanish mystic and Carmelite friar and one of the foremost poets of Spain. His writings, which reflect on the soul united to God in prayer, expressed in mystical terms, produced a profound poetry which has influenced the writers, philosophers and artists of the European tradition ever since. All his works, of which the best known are *The Spiritual Canticle* and *The Dark Night of the Soul*, are concerned with the same theme: the seeking of God by the soul in response to his love, and the painful experiences it endures on its way to spiritual maturity. They reflect the hardships of his own life, in particular his nine months imprisonment, but also the consolations he received at the same time. After one of his visions he made a pen and ink drawing of Christ on the Cross, which later provided the inspiration for Dali's masterpiece.

John had been incarcerated in a tiny room to which another room was attached and through which he eventually escaped. These rooms are reproduced in Viola's video, and the structural spaces of the construction, together with the Spanish texts of St John uttered by a voice from the inner room, provide the viewer of the work with a narrative framework which explains the situation. The subject matter is intelligible.

The video depicts a room within a room; an outer room accessible to all, which gives access to the inaccessible room of one's own interior. Outer and inner spaces are visually constructed which move us into the inner space of prayer. The artist uses imagery, space and sound to convey his meaning. Here, art not only documents the experience of prayer as the movement from the outward to the inward, but also makes it real, by our participation in the re-creation of the public and private experiences of St John himself. Prayer, like art, is not an affair of passivity, but a complex matter of space and time, of public and private: the public nature of life and faith and the private interiority of the personal relationship to God. Unlike Bernini's case, satisfaction is not immediate; interaction is offered by means of contemplation not impact, and the slow-motion technique is there to extend the gaze and to ponder on the mystery. As with John in his imprisonment, time is needed to absorb and understand our relationship with God.

III. Looking at the Author of the Faith

The double task of observation

The Fathers of the Church, and in particular St Augustine, were afraid of the ever-present danger in prayer of our ideas of God being simply turned into our own projections of him, and resulting in a distorted image of him. Our goal should be a simple, sincere and authentic image of ourselves before the true image of the True God. That is why the Fathers, Theodore Galle, together with the whole tradition, always see Christ as the model of ascent to God. Christ, besides being the perfect human being, is also, as the Council of Nicaea asserts, the consubstantial image of the Father, so that any prayer which is based on looking at him as the Author of the Faith can never lead astray the one who prays. If we look at him we shall experience what it means to be a true human being. By careful self-observation allied to careful observation of Christ we shall perceive God's care for us and his wisdom in our regard. And art has always proved to be one of the best aids in this double task of observation.

Vincent Van Gogh, Still Life with Bible. Van Gogh Museum, Amsterdam.

The path to God then passes through our own reality but the model for us is Christ, the unique image of God, but the one who shows himself to us according to our own unique apprehension, as Galle's woodcut reminds us. Galle also reminds us that while the image we have of Christ is rooted in the Bible, it is circumstance-orientated material. We receive the image of Christ as it is handed down in the text but the application of the picture to our own situation is shaped by our prayer.

Scripture and the human condition

VINCENT VAN GOGH expresses this very well in his *Still life with a Bible*, where the painting is dominated by the image of the Holy Scripture, the source of authority. Next to the Bible is an extinguished candle, a traditional feature in pictures of the still life genre known as memento mori. This very common genre was meant to emphasize the change and decay inherent in all things, and to provide for the observer a symbol of transience and death.

The juxtaposition with the Scripture however reminds us that the joy of the eternal is to be found out of the incipient decay. The idea is reinforced by the positioning in the foreground, but in a secondary role, of an old and well used copy of a modern French novel, Zola's *La Joie de Vivre*; the twelfth in the series of the

34

Les Rougon-Macquart novels, in which Zola wishes to show the effect on one family of hereditary and environmental factors. In the picture the novel represents a second authority: the authority of contemporary life, which contains its own wisdom, in its own way - for Zola's novels portray largely not the joy but the savagery and malevolence of life. Catholicism has never pretended that Christianity is simple; and the painting echoes this in its concrete visual presentation of spiritual values as ordered towards the realities of the human condition.

Van Gogh's bible is open at Isaiah 53 the ennobling of those who suffer. In the face of any situation, thought or feeling that might cause suffering or pain, we can oppose a positive way of thinking, based on reliable knowledge of God. The God of the Bible is the authoritative, positive Spirit who works through our current situation. Prayer is shown here as the struggle to achieve an integrated wisdom based on knowledge of two things: knowledge of Christ and knowledge of life.

Though separated by centuries Van Gogh's thinking is a recreation in visual terms of the doctrine of prayer found in one of the spiritual writers of the greatest influence in the history of spirituality. Evagrius of Pontus (346-399) wrote numerous and comprehensive works on spirituality which ever since have occupied a central place in the history of teaching on prayer. His books were read by an avid public whom he taught by means of short, pithy maxims, and he aimed at removing obstacles to prayer by starting from the position of psychology. In his *Antirrhetikos* he describes the soul under attack from what came later to be called the seven deadly sins. These vices can be overcome by opposing to them contrary (antirrhetic), positive expressions from the Bible. This antirrhetic method of prayer he regarded as being that of Christ himself, who set himself against the temptations of the Devil by giving contrary scriptural quotations. This confident way of thinking based on our familiar experience of God as he appears to us in the Scriptures gives us the vitality to cope with life.

The Annunciation and our tempting thoughts

The clearest representation of this approach – of thinking through a feeling or experience in order to reach God – is probably to be found above all in the commonest artistic image of the western world: the Annunciation, where the case represented is that of the deepest fear. The image of the Annunciation is a paradigm case for Christian prayer, and it is not surprising that it should have been so continuously depicted.

Most of the greatest representations of the Annunciation date from the period of the Renaissance, and of these some of the most beautiful are those created by **FRA ANGELICO**. His most exquisite is to be found in the corridor of the North Dormitory in the Convent of San Marco in Florence. The painting was meant to foster prayer and provide material both for the contemplation and delight of his Dominican brethren. The Virgin in the picture is a simple and unadorned girl, with an open face; an ordinary person not a medieval queen, who is beginning to realise that her life will be disrupted. Although she does not know the nature of the upheaval, she is prepared to trust God's providence.

All the images of the scene, as well as that of Van Gogh's more sophisticated presentation, can help us to analyse our own thoughts and feelings; and by inviting us into prayer they can help us to lose our imprisonment within our own problems. When faced in our prayer with a crisis which produces an incredibly strong feeling of antipathetic reaction, we can draw upon the Holy Spirit who, as the fourth century theologians St Basil, St Gregory of Nyssa and St Gregory Nazianzen describe him, is the positive energy of God. Put into the language of modern psychology, prayer based on the Bible is meant to be the true therapy for our problems and injuries, whether self-inflicted or otherwise; the wise direction of our personal psychological and physical energies; what we call emotional intelligence and what were called by St John Chrysostom, our *logismoi* (or assaultive or tempting thoughts).

Art and the image of Christ

When we obey the injunction of the epistle to the Hebrews and we look at the Author of our faith in our prayer we tend to feel very sure of what He looks like. The greatest artistic antirrhetic images, those which act on us to oppose negative thoughts and feelings, are the images which reveal to us the basic pattern of Christ's life as it is found in the Gospels.

These creations offer to our imagination an understanding of this pattern, and a means of discernment of it in our own lives. One of the fruits of the imagination is that it enables us to have the wisdom to reconcile the central values of the Gospel with those of our own unique personality. This is the general consideration on which St Ignatius Loyola based the principles for prayer in his celebrated *Spiritual Exercises*. And he is recorded as looking at an artistic print before he began his own prayer. St Ignatius's understanding of the imagination, as the innate ability to invent personal worlds within the mind from elements which we have gleaned from the realm of the senses, led him to think in images such as the two standards, and to offer the construction of imagery as a powerful means of prayer.

From the earlier centuries, when almost all European art was Christian art, we have inherited images of such astonishing quality and power, executed by artists of such extraordinary talent and imagination, that they have in turn shaped the imaginations of generations of their viewers. And it is for this reason that, despite the fact that we have no description visual or verbal of Christ's appearance, and we know Him only from the presentation in the Gospels, we have no difficulty in picturing Him.

The Good Shepherd

The earliest and most frequently represented image of Christ which we have and which, like the orans figures is found everywhere and in all artistic genres, is that of the *Good Shepherd* on the cover of this book. A fresco from the Catacomb of Callixtus dating from the third century provides a beautiful and typical example. The composition has two main elements: a frontal standing figure of a youthful shepherd, clad in a short tunic and carrying his milk pail, and flanked by two relaxed and happy sheep, representing his token flock, within a grove of leafy trees. The bucolic and pastoral nature of the scene is reinforced by the added depiction of some birds.

Statuettes of shepherds were common as garden ornaments in pagan villas and houses, where they represented a romantic and paradisal idea of the bucolic way of life. They also served as reminders of the solid worth accruing from good husbandry. So while the image of the Good Shepherd is iconographically derived from an environment in which shepherding was a typical and important feature of everyday life, and one with which the artist could assume his viewers to have been thoroughly familiar, for Christians the Good Shepherd was a biblical figure. The picture is thus related to the text in a symbolic way by means of a representation derived from current stock. The image is at one and the same time a scriptural and symbolic figure and also a figure of real life. So he becomes the archetypal image of Christ as the Saviour, who sets up a personal relationship of care for his followers through their incorporation into his flock. For the earliest Christians, looking at the Author of the Faith in their prayer meant having a sense of security based on the knowledge of his saving love, and the power and strength of his protection.

The realism of a crucified Christ

For medieval Christians on the other hand the image of Christ is related to the Scripture in a much more realistic way, though without ever degenerating into mere illustration. For them looking at the Author of the Faith meant seeing his saving love exemplified primarily in his suffering on the cross. And ever since the medieval period, art has taught us to think of Christ less symbolically and more realistically The generic image created in the early period has now become more specific. Medieval imagery achieves the combination of uniting the historic and realistic narration of the passion with at the same time an emphasis on its personal application.

Classic in this respect is the *Isenheim Altarpiece*, now in Colmar in Alsace, one of the most famous western representations in existence of the crucifixion. This altarpiece, made just before the Reformation - when it first escaped destruction, and again a second time when it was saved from the fury of the French Revolution - is one of the most outstanding products of the Catholic imagination. The superb quality of the execution, the amazing content of the imagery, and its extraordinary complexity have combined to turn it into one of the most widely acknowledged masterpieces of Christian art, which the western world now takes for granted as part of its Judaeo- Christian heritage. Once seen it is unforgettable, and it has preoccupied painters and composers of the modern era such as Picasso and Hindemith. It always touches the present condition, and it is one of those rare images like the *Maesta* of Duccio which, once seen, exercise an effective influence in the life of its viewer.

Created between 1512 and 1516 by the German artist universally known as **MATTHIAS GRÜNEWALD**, it was commissioned by the Antonites, a medical order, for the chapel of their hospital and monastery at Isenheim. This order, whose patron saint was St Anthony Abbot, was particularly dedicated to the care of those suffering from the so-called St Anthony's Fire, an incurable skin disease causing immense pain, and the symptoms of which are shown all over the body of the dying Christ in the image. It has two sets of folding wings, and when the altarpiece is in its normal closed state, it is the scene of the crucifixion which is displayed. When the outermost wings are opened a corresponding resurrection scene is revealed.

The crucifixion shows in harrowing detail the contorted and lacerated figure of Christ suffering the dual agony of death by crucifixion and death by St Anthony's Fire. On the left is his Mother, arching and fainting back from the horror of the scene, being

Mathias Grünewald, Crucifixion from the Isenheim Altarpiece, Unterlinden Museum, Colmar.

supported by John the Apostle, with Mary Magdalene kneeling at the foot of the cross in prayer. On the right is John the Baptist, who historically had died before these events, pointing with an extraordinarily long index finger to the dying Saviour. At his feet is a lamb holding a cross. The lamb and the elongated finger indicate with incredible visual economy the doctrinal meaning of the death – Christ dies as a sacrifice for all human beings – but the inflamed sores show that pain, being an individual and private experience, is identified with it and given divine significance through it.

The altarpiece shows with devastating clarity what deviation from human health and well being really means. And it has a modern artistic parallel in the whole genre of art that resulted from the plague of the aids virus; especially in the ghostly representations of Daniel Goldstein, with their invocations of the Shroud of Turin. Both the altarpiece and the *Reliquaries*, as Goldstein calls them, convey the primacy of the personal through a conventional and traditionally established format. Although based on the Gospel, the impact of the altarpiece relates directly to the visual perception of the viewer. What can be experienced and identified with comes directly from seeing rather than from the words of the Scripture text.

44

The resurrection scene

The same is true of the resurrection scene. While the crucifixion is livid and sombre, the resurrection is a scene of glory and brilliant colour and light. Christ's body, which had been covered in wounds is transmuted into a blaze of the alabaster translucence of a light that appears to come from within itself. The body on the cross had its boundaries clearly delineated, but here, due to the incredible skill of the artist, it is impossible to separate the body from the light around it while still being able to distinguish it. For Grunewald's sick viewers, if their disease was a comparable testing of a religious commitment which required enduring faith, then this freedom and resurrection is the result obtained for them no less than for Christ.

For this reason Grünewald had included among the imagery of his altarpiece some words from the *Golden Legend*, which gives a popular account of the life of Anthony. It records him as praying in temptation: "where were you, good Jesus, where were you? Why were you not there to heal my wounds?" The answer lies in the resurrection scene, where the personal transcendence of his sufferings by Christ in his supremely loving act, is the guarantee of their own transcendence, and of his presence and reassuring hope to those who look upon the Author of their Faith.

Hayum, who has studied the image in detail, points out that the fundamental message is not only a promise of future good health and the end of suffering but goes beyond it, to the promise of a place in heaven. Grünewald's approach to the condition of disease and pain is to show it as the revelation of a future life.

His work shows us too the relation of the Scripture and art, word and image, to prayer. While the Scripture and its account of Christ underlies and supports everything, the expression is the artist's and our own interpretation. It is the image and our perception which embodies and brings to life the sense and the mood of the text. Likewise all can find a desired image for picturing their own understanding of Christ and their personal relationship to him in the long and richly illustrated representation of the incidents of the New Testament which are found in the western artistic tradition.

A more environmental direction

Often we do not need human or disturbing and violent images to bring the same ideas before our minds. In the sixteenth-century the Council of Trent, moving away from the depiction of the crucifixion, generated an image which expresses the same ideas but in a more environmental direction, which perhaps resonates more readily with a twenty first-century understanding and sensibility. This is the image of the host surrounded by a garland of flowers. It is based on the classical genre of the still life, the purpose of which is to concentrate attention on the idea itself by removing any reference to living being.

Sometimes a motif drawn from nature can become simply emblematic, as with the case of the sunflower. St Julie, whom we referred to earlier, once remarked that the soul at prayer is like a sunflower, which according to legend, follows all the movements of the sun, from which it receives the warmth that vivifies it and the light that guides it. And, in an iconographically complicated illustration from an eighteenth-century manuscript belonging to the Benedictine Abbey of Melk in Austria, a giant sunflower is shown bending over the Abbey while this time it receives rain from a cloud on which are seated five saints. In the same way Van Gogh's *Sunflowers* were meant to entrap and pass on to us the light and warmth of the French south and its strong sun. We know from his letters, which provide a running commentary on his painting, that, for Van Gogh, Christ was the personification of his own view of the world. The ability to enjoy and delight in God's creation in prayer, whether through nature itself, a landscape or a still life, is the attitude which receives all from God: the beatitude, which calls the poor in spirit, blessed.

Art, prayer and the aesthetic

Looking at the Author of the Faith then is not just one experience in a theological system; it is the controlling experience which unifies everything. And since prayer is the response to his divine attractiveness, the life of prayer is fundamentally and theologically speaking aesthetic. Beauty is for most of us a real universal value of great importance, which shapes how we live, although no-one has ever been able to offer a final definition of it. We tend to speak of it in two ways: of outer beauty, which is a characteristic of the appearance of some person or object, and inner beauty which refers to the psychological factors inherent in the personality. As we know famously from Kant, it is a matter of taste, and so it is a subjective experience and a subjective judgment. Great beauty therefore can exist with immorality, or as St Augustine put it, it is a gift given by God to the wicked as well as the good, and thus it can be not only a matter of ambiguity but of evil. One of the problems concerning the films of Leni Riefenstahl is raised by this paradox, in that the beauty of their art was used to glorify Nazi ideology.

Although it was an idea adopted by the Pythagoreans, whose interest in mathematics led them to value order and symmetry and to study music, it was developed by Plato as a philosophical concept and from him passed to

Christianity. Despite its ambiguity, Christian theology has always regarded beauty as a final and primary value; and – except for isolated periods of iconoclasm – in its concern to describe the nature and attraction of God as divine love, has always adopted the language of aesthetics, and par excellence, the language of art.

The New Testament had described Christ as the light of the world, and light and its nature came to be considered as the most beautiful revelation of the ideal beauty of God. And likewise the question of the representation of light and its effects has always been a preoccupation for artists, particularly for the Impressionists. For the medieval period it was exemplified in the construction of stained glass. It was the play of light on the gold and jewels in the Abbey's treasury that led Abbot Suger, according to his own account, into developing the glories of Gothic architecture and art. He was preoccupied with splendour and beauty, and referred to God as the Father of Lights, Christ as the First Radiance and his people as the Smaller Lights. For Suger the whole universe was constructed on beauty, reflecting the ideal beauty of God.

Viewpoint

Beauty as art presents it to us is concerned with appearances. And Scruton remarks that the image helps us to frame the appearance of the person we love. It offers us an representation which looks right to us and so we can prefer one image rather than another. In studying the appearance of Christ we are examining those aspects in him which render him personally attractive to us; and the images we choose for prayer are a matter of highly subjective choice. They provide for us a very personal apprehension and experience of pleasure, justification and fulfilment.

Beauty however has a social dimension in that some artistic masterpieces seem to portray the attractiveness of God so perfectly, for so many people, that they have a universal and enduring appeal. One of the most celebrated illustrations of this phenomenon is **SALVADOR DALI'S** *Christ of Saint John of the Cross*. It is one of the most famous and most commercial images of all time.

Dali (1904-1959) was moved to create his masterpiece on seeing St John of the Cross's drawing in which he had translated his visions of Christ into art form. Originally dismissed as yet another of Dali's stunts, it has become one of the world's favourite paintings, because the extravagance for which Dali's paintings had become famous is here constrained by the subject matter. He once said that photography had become the salvation of painting, and the image does somewhat resemble a colour photograph in its almost extravagant

Salvador Dali, Christ of Saint John of the Cross, Kelvingrove Art Gallery and Museum, Glasgow.

realism. We see every detail of Christ's curly head, and it is very beautiful in a traditional way. The significance of the crucifixion is told from the Father's point of view and so the angle of the cross and the crucified Christ are striking. There is a great contrast of light and dark and the painting impresses deeply by the aesthetic treatment of its surface effects. Dali wrote that he considered the picture to represent "the very unity of the universe, the Christ." And for many people it is the visual summary of God's redemptive love for the human race. Despite the ugliness of the real, historical passion, by the beauty of its portrayal here the painting reveals the Father's value system at the heart of the universe. It exists beyond but also within the conditions of our existence, time and space. God is nothing more or less than overflowing goodness; God, as the fourth Gospel says, is love.

IV. Conclusion

Frameworks for Art and Prayer

In this study we have tried to offer a critical and reflective approach to the traditional practice of expressing ideas concerning God and his relationship to ourselves and the world by means of artistic expression. And in this area, because of its multivalent nature, art has proved to be a reliable way of opening up the wider questions central to our lives and our experience of God. It has appeared to be a particularly fruitful approach, in that it has provided a framework for considering art and prayer in this day and age, as we live in a world which is increasingly dominated by the visual image, and one in which art becomes evermore culturally dominant. The verbal means of expression is no longer given the premium which it has had for so long especially in European thinking. Other ranges of thought and imagination are necessary for prayer in contemporary society.

In reflecting back on the material we have studied, several conclusions present themselves. First as we have seen there is no one single or separate explanatory description which can do justice to the whole idea;

because the basic engagement in both cases is not with any given image but with the model which the images represent: Christ. No one definition of either art or prayer can do justice to our relationship with him.

Framework of tradition

Nevertheless with this proviso, we have discovered several frameworks into which the whole issue of art and prayer can be put. In the first place Pope Paul VI himself located the largest framework, in that he showed that both art and prayer must take place within the tradition of the Church; and further that within the tradition art must retain its autonomy. In this he was echoing St Gregory the Great who wrote in one of his letters that we do nothing wrong in wishing to show the invisible by means of the visible.

This preservation of both tradition and autonomy is possible because images are by their nature ambiguous rather than true or false, and so no question of orthodoxy or heresy can be applied to them as in the case of doctrinal propositions. For the early and medieval Church art was the visual interpretation of doctrine; and the Faith and its Author could often be depicted by artists in ways that do not always echo the conventional expressions as they are found in the literary statements of the Creed and the Definitions. The artistic idiom develops the faith in a noncontroversial way since the images function by means of personal response and not as with the written word by means of logic. So issues of truth or non-truth do not arise in this context. Art depends for its validity not on proof of argument but on satisfying the hearts and imaginations of its consumers. An interesting historical fact is that art has always been the authentic voice of the laity in the articulation of the tradition, and it has always been an area which has been remarkably free from official control. It places in the hand of the Christian at prayer a powerful tool for the expression of one's traditional faith. While the only reaction to images is of response and non-response, they can and do serve to heighten our awareness of doctrine and our consciousness of its importance and intensity in our life with God.

Framework of creativity

A second conceptual framework arises from the particular works which were selected and the material we reviewed: the framework of creativity. We examined a number of images from the artistic tradition which belong to various artists, various genres and various historical periods. This has allowed us to see the need for a structure for prayer which is composed of different voices and approaches, and different forms of creativity and imagination. For Catholics creativity is a basic category both naturally human and culturally constructed, because it has its origins in God whose nature is creative. Though the nature of the creative process itself is highly unclear, it produces in the world a real manifestation of the presence of God by means of human activity. Most fields of human industry value creativity, whether it is the arts and media, science, medicine, technology, economics etc. Since its character is innovative, it often goes against existing ideas and values, and one definition of creativity is that it is a process which overturns assumptions. This is true also of prayer, and what we have seen at work in these images is first of all freedom; a freedom which echoes and feeds the freedom before God of the person at prayer.

Framework of subject matter

This leads thirdly to the framework of subject matter. We have seen that images for prayer do not have to be figurative or representational in any way. Religious issues can arise from seemingly very secular works because images for prayer are neither documentary nor descriptive but informative, when they concern Christ and the human being. When one image stands out by virtue of its positive differences from other images, we focus on how it represents rather than on what it represents. It presents biblical values not so much by subject matter but by a relation of kinship. Abstraction and video art have endowed this relationship with a new sense of purpose and have illuminated the meaning and content of the Scripture in a new way. They interpret the Christian faith in a new way by establishing in some way a connection to the so-called zeitgeist, the notion of the spirit of a given time. While we have seen an exchange of ideas and imagery between art and Scripture, our examination has shown that art has gone further in the development of biblical meaning. It is art which carries into the specific area of our life the universal teachings of the Bible.

The framework of the aesthetic

Fourthly and allied to this, is the discovery that not all images are suitable for prayer. It is the faith of the Church and the need of the person praying which provides the criterion and interrogates the usefulness of the image in this context. This leads on to a matter which we have seen to be of crucial significance to our issue, the central importance of aesthetic considerations. The framework of the aesthetic cannot be overestimated in matters of art and prayer.

Within the history of art over the last hundred years the idea of beauty had become derided, but during the last ten years the position has begun to change, and we find in the literature a call for a renewed attention to beauty as a significant issue in contemporary life and contemporary art. In many recent studies an enquiry into its nature, and the corresponding notion of ugliness, and a re-appraisal of their conceptual usefulness has come to the fore. In our study the question of beauty occurred in the context of its habitual appearance within the Christian tradition. For Christian art the paradox of beauty, shining forth through the ugliness of the cross and crucifixion, has always presented a challenge to representation, as we have seen. The works we have examined show that it is a challenge to which art has risen triumphantly, providing nourishment for prayer.

The concept of the aesthetic clarifies for us the nature of the criterion to which we made reference above; and it offers us also the question which we must put to any given representation: does this object or artefact lead us to knowledge and love of Christ? Can we see in it a reference to the Author of the Faith? All the images with which we have been concerned are works of the greatest originality, creative masterpieces of the Western tradition, and they have answered the question in the affirmative. What however should we do with images, albeit showing explicitly Christian subject matter, but which most people would regard as kitsch?

Kitsch is the German word for art considered to be inferior or tasteless or stylistically worthless. The question arose as a controversy within the French Catholicism in the middle of the twentieth-century. It concerned the so-called "holy pictures" offered in churches as aids to devotion. These pictures were the results of nineteenth-century industrial production, and though they answered a popular demand, in artistic terms they were very shallow. They reproduced in large numbers an imitation 'at a low level' of art that was of real value. The problem with such images for prayer in comparison with the representations we have studied is that the latter, like prayer, demand effort and engagement in order to discover Christ. Both looking at pictures and engaging in prayer require an active participation and a certain amount of discipline. The "kitsch" images on the other hand are simply received as passive. They stop at the level of sentimentality rather than sentiment and of superficiality rather than intellectual depth. They are mechanical rather than artistic and what they offer is an aesthetic based on artifice. What they offer is beauty without truth.

It was Keats who declared that beauty is synonymous with truth and, though his famous aphorism is difficult to interpret, he seems to mean that images of genuine artistic value, by helping us to perceive the persons or things we love, assist us to go further and establish what we actually think about them. Although the link of beauty and morality may be conceptually difficult to establish, these images in particular show a visual connection between the ideas of beauty, truth and goodness through the concept of love. They show the power of images to function in our thinking on a level well beyond the purely intellectual. Scruton says that our favourite works of art seem to guide us to truth by being concrete examples of things, which like ourselves, are worthwhile simply by their own intrinsic existence. The inspirational quality of real world objects offers us an example of the interplay of truth, beauty and goodness which are found fully integrated in the creative nature of God. So in matters of prayer we cannot do without them.

The environment

Finally there is the framework of the environment: the constants and variables of human life. During the centuries of change which we have observed some things in life remain as constants – birth, death, personal relationships, the need of supportive surroundings - other things change along with historical and cultural need. Art like prayer deals with these constants and variables of human life. It shows the universalities that constitute being human by means of displaying the concreteness of any given time. As Bernini showed us, no universal meaning can be conveyed without the relativity that the concreteness of the artwork implies. This paradox of the transcending character of art to communicate across the centuries to a contemporary environment from which it is very different, and yet with which it appears contemporaneous, appears little short of miraculous. It is the aspect of art which places it in the realm of affirmation, and which endows it with a kind of prophetic ability that nourishes prayer. Significant art conveys more than what has transpired at a given time; from that given time it carries us into an illumination of humanity in our own time. It lays bare meaningful aspects of our own life which might otherwise we might have missed, and so becomes for us a source of the transformation which we hope to achieve through prayer.

Christian life as art

By starting out from the consideration of particular examples it has been possible to gain some sense of the whole relationship of art to prayer, and to understand how best to gain accessibility to the realm of the spirit by turning to the work of artists. These perspectives on art have perhaps taught us to think of the Christian life itself as a work of art. No work of art is more important than our own life, and we are all artists in this sense. Like the object created by the artist, our lives are meant to convey the truth, beauty and love expressed by the genuine work of art. But the Christian life as we experience it is not finished; it is constantly a work in progress, constantly corrected or moved forward and finally accomplished by our prayer. The work of art happens when there is an adequate correspondence between form and content, so the quality of the work will depend on the quality of our prayer.

As Christians, when day by day we study in our prayer the Author of the Faith and attempt to reproduce in our lives the model he offers, we begin to see the emergence of our true self-portrait, the image of the creator God himself, the Supreme Artist.

Bibliography

J.Ethrington *The Church and Art* (Address of Pope Paul VI and reply of Sir John Rothenstein, decrees of II Vatican Council on sacred art) St Aidan's R.C. Church, 1964

J. Spier *Picturing the Bible* Yale University Press, 2007 (Early Christian Art)

A. Hayum *God's Medicine and the Painter's Vision* Princeton University Press, (date not known) (The Isenheim Altarpiece)

M. Snodin and N. Llewellyn edd. *Baroque 1620-1800* Victoria and Albert Museum, 2009 (Bernini)

B. Thomson *Van Gogh Paintings* Thames and Hudson, (no date given)

J. Golding *Paths to the Absolute* Thames and Hudson, 2000 (Rothko and Newman)

M. Rush *New Media in Art* Thames and Hudson, 2005 (Cinema, Video, Digital)

C. Townsend ed. *The Art of Bill Viola* Thames and Hudson, 2004

R. Gomez de la Serna *Dali* Wellfleet Press, 2003

C. Lyas *Aesthetics* UCL Press, 1997

R. Scruton *Beauty* OUP, 2009